Metsology
Trivia
Challenge

New York Mets Baseball

Metsology
Trivia
Challenge

New York Mets Baseball

Researched by Al Netzer

Paul F. Wilson & Tom P. Rippey III, Editors

Kick The Ball, Ltd
Lewis Center, Ohio

Trivia by Kick The Ball, Ltd

College Football Trivia

Alabama Crimson Tide	Auburn Tigers	Boston College Eagles	Florida Gators
Georgia Bulldogs	LSU Tigers	Miami Hurricanes	Michigan Wolverines
Nebraska Cornhuskers	Notre Dame Fighting Irish	Ohio State Buckeyes	Oklahoma Sooners
Oregon Ducks	Penn State Nittany Lions	Southern Cal Trojans	Texas Longhorns

Pro Football Trivia

Arizona Cardinals	Buffalo Bills	Chicago Bears	Cleveland Browns
Denver Broncos	Green Bay Packers	Indianapolis Colts	Kansas City Chiefs
Minnesota Vikings	New England Patriots	Oakland Raiders	Pittsburgh Steelers
San Francisco 49ers	Washington Redskins		

Pro Baseball Trivia

Boston Red Sox	Chicago Cubs	Chicago White Sox	Cincinnati Reds
Detroit Tigers	Los Angeles Dodgers	New York Mets	New York Yankees
Philadelphia Phillies	Saint Louis Cardinals	San Francisco Giants	

College Basketball Trivia

Duke Blue Devils	Georgetown Hoyas	Indiana Hoosiers	Kansas Jayhawks
Kentucky Wildcats	Maryland Terrapins	Michigan State Spartans	North Carolina Tar Heels
Syracuse Orange	UConn Huskies	UCLA Bruins	

Pro Basketball Trivia

Boston Celtics	Chicago Bulls	Detroit Pistons	Los Angeles Lakers
Utah Jazz			

Visit **www.TriviaGameBooks.com** for more details.

This book is dedicated to our families and friends for your unwavering love, support, and your understanding of our pursuit of our passions. Thank you for everything you do for us and for making our lives complete.

Metsology Trivia Challenge: New York Mets Baseball;
First Edition 2010

Published by
Kick The Ball, Ltd
8595 Columbus Pike, Suite 197
Lewis Center, OH 43035
www.TriviaGameBooks.com

Designed, Formatted, and Edited by: Paul F. Wilson & Tom P. Rippey III
Researched by: Al Netzer

*For information on ordering this book in bulk at reduced prices, please email us
at pfwilson@triviagamebooks.com.*

International Standard Book Number: 978-1-934372-82-1

Printed and Bound in the United States of America

10 9 8 7 6 5 4 3 2 1

Table of Contents

Dear Friend,

Thank you for purchasing our *Metsology Trivia Challenge* game book!

We have made every attempt to verify the accuracy of the questions and answers contained in this book. However it is still possible that from time to time an error has been made by us or our researchers. In the event you find a question or answer that is questionable or inaccurate, we ask for your understanding and thank you for bringing it to our attention so we may improve future editions of this book. Please email us at tprippey@triviagamebooks.com with those observations and comments.

Have fun playing *Metsology Trivia Challenge*!

Paul and Tom

Paul Wilson and Tom Rippey
Co-Founders, Kick The Ball, Ltd

PS – You can discover more about all of our current trivia game books by visiting www.TriviaGameBooks.com.

Book Format:

There are four quarters, each made up of fifty questions. Each quarter's questions have assigned point values. Questions are designed to get progressively more difficult as you proceed through each quarter, as well as through the book itself. Most questions are in a four-option multiple-choice format so that you will at least have a 25% chance of getting a correct answer for some of the more challenging questions.

We have even added extra innings in the event of a tie, or just in case you want to keep playing a little longer.

Game Options:

One Player -
To play on your own, simply answer each of the questions in all the quarters, and in the overtime section, if you'd like. Use the Player / Team Score Sheet to record your answers and the quarter Answer Keys to check your answers. Calculate each quarter's points and the total for the game at the bottom of the Player / Team Score Sheet to determine your final score.

Two or More Players –
To play with multiple players decide if you will all be competing with each other individually, or if you will form and play as teams. Each player / team will then have its own Player / Team Score Sheet to record its answer. You can use the quarter Answer Keys to check your answers and to calculate your final scores.

How to Play
Metsology Trivia Challenge

The Player / Team Score Sheets have been designed so that each team can answer all questions or you can divide the questions up in any combination you would prefer. For example, you may want to alternate questions if two players are playing or answer every third question for three players, etc. In any case, simply record your response to your questions in the corresponding quarter and question number on the Player / Team Score Sheet.

A winner will be determined by multiplying the total number of correct answers for each quarter by the point value per quarter, then adding together the final total for all quarters combined. Play the game again and again by alternating the questions that your team is assigned so that you will answer a different set of questions each time you play.

You Create the Game -
There are countless other ways of using *Metsology Trivia Challenge* questions. It is limited only to your imagination. Examples might be using them at your tailgate or other professional baseball related party. Players / Teams who answer questions incorrectly may have to perform a required action, or winners may receive special prizes. Let us know what other games you come up with!

Have fun!

1) What year was the nickname Mets officially
adopted by New York?

Answers begin on page 17

    A)   1960
    B)   1961
    C)   1964
    D)   1966

2) What are the Mets' official colors?

    A)   Orange and Blue
    B)   Purple and Blue
    C)   Orange, Royal Blue, and Black
    D)   White, Blue, and Black

3) What is the name of the Mets' current home stadium?

    A)   Citi Field
    B)   The Meadowlands
    C)   Shea Stadium
    D)   Citibank Park

4) What year did the Mets join the National League?

    A)   1959
    B)   1961
    C)   1962
    D)   1964

5) What years did Willie Mays play for the Mets?

    A)   1968-69
    B)   1970-71
    C)   1972-73
    D)   1975-76

6) In which National League division do the Mets play?

    A)   Central
    B)   Northeast
    C)   West
    D)   East

7) When was the most recent season the Mets won 100 or more games?

    A)   1969
    B)   1986
    C)   1988
    D)   2006

8) Who has managed the most Mets games?

    A)   Gil Hodges
    B)   Joe Torre
    C)   Willie Randolph
    D)   Davey Johnson

9) From which team did the Mets receive Johan Santana?

    A) Washington Nationals
    B) Minnesota Twins
    C) Seattle Mariners
    D) Pittsburgh Pirates

10) What is the name of the Mets' mascot?

    A) Mr. Met
    B) Big Apple
    C) Lady Met
    D) Captain Met

11) Who was the Mets' opponent in their most recent World Series appearance?

    A) Chicago White Sox
    B) Boston Red Sox
    C) New York Yankees
    D) Oakland Athletics

12) The Mets have never turned a triple play in their history.

    A) True
    B) False

13) What is the Mets' theme song?

    A) "Meet the Mets"
    B) "Our Team, Our Time"
    C) "Let's Go Mets Go"
    D) "Get Metsmerized"

14) Which Met was nicknamed "The Franchise"?

    A) Jerry Koosman
    B) Keith Hernandez
    C) Mookie Wilson
    D) Tom Seaver

15) New York's stadium has a seating capacity over 50,000.

    A) True
    B) False

16) Who is the Mets' current manager?

    A) Willie Randolph
    B) Omar Minaya
    C) Jerry Manuel
    D) Sandy Alomar Sr.

17) Who did the Mets play in their final series of 2009?

A)   Houston Astros
B)   Atlanta Braves
C)   Washington Nationals
D)   Florida Marlins

18) What year did the Mets play in their first-ever World Series?

A)   1966
B)   1969
C)   1973
D)   1986

19) Who holds the Mets' career record for games pitched?

A)   Tom Seaver
B)   Jerry Koosman
C)   John Franco
D)   Dwight Gooden

20) Who hit the most home runs for the Mets in 2009?

A)   Jeff Francoeur
B)   Carlos Beltran
C)   Gary Sheffield
D)   Daniel Murphy

21) Which team entered the National League the same year as the Mets?

    A)   San Diego Padres
    B)   Montreal Expos
    C)   Houston Colt .45s
    D)   Colorado Rockies

22) What year did the Mets win their first-ever postseason game?

    A)   1964
    B)   1966
    C)   1967
    D)   1969

23) How many total runs did the Mets score in the 2009 regular season?

    A)   671
    B)   707
    C)   730
    D)   776

24) Did the Mets win greater than 95 games in the 2009 regular season?

    A)   Yes
    B)   No

25) How many times has a Mets pitcher recorded four strikeouts in an inning?

    A) 2
    B) 3
    C) 5
    D) 6

26) Who was credited with first using "The Amazin' Mets", the popular nickname from the 1969 season?

    A) Tom Seaver
    B) Gil Hodges
    C) Bob Murphy
    D) Casey Stengel

27) Who was the most recent Met to win a Cy Young Award?

    A) Bobby Jones
    B) Dwight Gooden
    C) Tom Seaver
    D) Johan Santana

28) Who is the only Mets player to ever have a six-hit game?

    A) Mike Piazza
    B) George Foster
    C) Keith Hernandez
    D) Edgardo Alfonzo

29) Mets closer Tug McGraw came up with the 1973 Mets rallying cry "You Gotta Believe!".

    A) True
    B) False

30) What is the largest deficit the Mets have overcome to win a game?

    A) 7 points
    B) 8 points
    C) 10 points
    D) 11 points

31) How many times has a Mets pitcher won 20 or more games?

    A) 5
    B) 6
    C) 8
    D) 10

32) How many times have the Mets won 100 or more games in a season?

    A) 1
    B) 3
    C) 4
    D) 7

33) What year did the Home Run Apple make its debut?

    A) 1962
    B) 1969
    C) 1976
    D) 1980

34) What is the Mets' record for consecutive games with a safe hit?

    A) 21
    B) 24
    C) 30
    D) 33

35) Did the Mets have a winning record at the midseason break in 2009?

    A) Yes
    B) No

36) Which Mets pitcher had the most wins in 2009?

    A) Livan Hernandez
    B) Mike Pelfrey
    C) John Maine
    D) Johan Santana

37) Who is the only Mets pitcher to hit two home runs in the same game?

  A) Walt Terrell
  B) Jack Hamilton
  C) John Maine
  D) Steve Trachsel

38) Against which National League team did the Mets have the highest winning percentage during the 2009 regular season?

  A) Cincinnati Reds
  B) San Francisco Giants
  C) Washington Nationals
  D) Colorado Rockies

39) How many all-time World Series have the Mets won?

  A) 1
  B) 2
  C) 3
  D) 5

40) What was Dwight Gooden's nickname while playing for the Mets?

  A) Doc
  B) Lord Charles
  C) Sweetness
  D) D-Man

41) Which Met had the most RBIs in the 2006 National League Championship Series?

    A)   Carlos Beltran
    B)   Jose Reyes
    C)   Carlos Delgado
    D)   David Wright

42) How many times have the Mets scored greater than 800 runs in a season?

    A)   4
    B)   5
    C)   7
    D)   10

43) Which of the following pitchers threw the most one-hit complete games as a Met?

    A)   Tom Seaver
    B)   Tom Glavine
    C)   David Cone
    D)   Dwight Gooden

44) How many Mets were selected to the 2009 All-Star team?

    A)   2
    B)   4
    C)   5
    D)   7

45) Which Mets player holds the record for most grand slams in a month?

    A)   John Milner
    B)   Robin Ventura
    C)   Mike Piazza
    D)   Carlos Beltran

46) What are the most Mets selected as All-Stars in a single season?

    A)   4
    B)   6
    C)   7
    D)   8

47) How many Mets managers lasted one season or less?

    A)   4
    B)   6
    C)   9
    D)   13

48) How many hits did the Mets pitching staff have in 2009?

    A)   22
    B)   29
    C)   37
    D)   48

49) What is the nickname of the AAA team affiliated with the New York Mets?

    A)   Buffalo Bisons
    B)   Savannah Sand Gnats
    C)   St. Lucie Mets
    D)   Binghamton Mets

50) When was the first season the New York Mets had a winning record against the Atlanta Braves?

    A)   1964
    B)   1967
    C)   1969
    D)   1975

The Mets' first old-timers game was held on July 14, 1962, when the team was less than a year old. The game featured players from New York's past, namely the Brooklyn Dodgers and New York Giants of 1951. It was a rematch of the famous "Shot Heard 'Round the World" game, in which the Giants' Bobby Thomson hit a walk-off home run off of the Dodgers' Ralph Branca to win the National League pennant. In the rematch, with 37,253 fans watching, Thompson connected on a 2-2 pitch from Branca. The crowd jumped to their feet only to watch Duke Snider catch a routine fly ball in center field. The new franchise, by honoring one of the greatest moments in sports, showed they cared about the rich history of New York baseball.

Spring Training / Answer Key
Metsology Trivia Challenge

1) B – 1961 (It is a natural shortening of the name of an earlier baseball club called the New York Metropolitans that played in the 1880s.)

2) C – Orange, Royal Blue, and Black (The original colors were Orange and Royal Blue. Black was added as an additional color in 1998.)

3) A – Citi Field (The Mets opened the 2009 regular season in their new ballpark. The stadium's construction costs totaled $800 million.)

4) B – 1961 (On March 6, 1961, Warren Giles, National League President at the time, officially welcomed the Mets into the NL.)

5) C – 1972-73 (Willie was traded to the Mets in May of 1972. He hit a game-winning home run against his former team, the San Francisco Giants, in his Mets debut.)

6) D – East (Other teams in the division include the Atlanta Braves, Florida Marlins, Philadelphia Phillies, and Washington Nationals.)

7) C – 1988 (The Mets finished with a 100-60 record.)

8) D – Davey Johnson (Johnson managed 1,012 games for the Mets from 1984-90.)

9) B – Minnesota Twins (The Mets acquired Santana on Feb. 2, 2008, in exchange for four players.)

10) A – Mr. Met (One of the first mascots in Major League Baseball to appear in costumed form [1964], he was introduced to fans on the covers of game programs a year earlier.)

11) C – New York Yankees (The Mets lost the 2000 World Series 1-4 to the Yankees.)

12) B – False (The Mets have turned 8 triple plays. The most recent occurred on May 17, 2002, against the San Diego Padres.)

13) A – "Meet the Mets" (Written in 1961 by Ruth Roberts and Bill Katz, it is played during a break in late innings at Citi Field as a crowd sing-along.)

14) D – Tom Seaver (The Mets won a special lottery with three other teams for the right to sign Seaver in 1966.)

15) B – False (The stadium has a seating capacity of 41,800.)

16) C – Jerry Manuel (He has been the Mets' manager since the middle of the 2008 season.)

17) A – Houston Astros (The Mets swept their three-game series with the Astros at Citi Field.)

18) B – 1969 (The Mets won the Series 4-1 against the Baltimore Orioles. Future Mets manager Davey Johnson played second base for the Orioles.)

19) C – John Franco (Franco holds the record with 695 games pitched [1990-2004].)

20) A – Jeff Francoeur (He led the team with 15 home runs.)

21) C – Houston Colt .45s (The team was renamed the Astros in 1965.)

22) D – 1969 (The Mets swept the Atlanta Braves 3-0 in the National League Championship Series.)

23) A – 671 (The Mets scored 671 runs off of 1,472 hits.)

24) B – No (The Mets finished the season with a record of 70-92, for a .432 winning percentage.)

25) A – 2 (Two Mets have accomplished this feat, Derek Wallace in 1996 against Atlanta and Mike Stanton in 2004 against Milwaukee. This happens when a third strike is not cleanly caught by the catcher and the runner reaches base. The third strikeout is still recorded.)

26) D – Casey Stengel (The Mets' first-ever manager used to refer to the team as 'Amazin' when he managed the team from 1962-64.)

27) B – Dwight Gooden (He won the award in 1985 at the age of 20, becoming the youngest pitcher to win the Cy Young Award.)

28) D – Edgardo Alfonzo (He had six hits, including three home runs and a double, against the Astros on Aug. 30, 1999.)

29) A – True (In August of 1973 when the Mets were in last place, a fan asked Tug McGraw, "What's wrong with the Mets?" Tug replied, "There's nothing wrong with the Mets. You gotta believe!" The Mets came from 9.5 games back to win the division and the NL Pennant.)

30) B – 8 points (The Mets trailed the Astros 0-8 after seven innings. They scored seven runs in the eighth and four more in the ninth to win 11-8.)

31) C – 8 (The most recent Mets pitcher to have 20 wins in a season was Frank Viola in 1990 [20-12].)

32) B – 3 (1969 [100-62], 1986 [108-54], and 1988 [100-60])

33) D – 1980 (The original Home Run Apple at Shea Stadium weighed 582 pounds, while the new one at Citi Field weighs about 8,500 pounds.)

34) C – 30 (Moises Alou set this record from Aug. 23, 2007 to Sept. 26, 2007.)

35) B – No (The Mets had a record of 42-45, for a .483 winning percentage.)

36) D – Johan Santana (Santana finished with a 13-9 record.)

37) A – Walt Terrell (Walt hit two home runs against the Chicago Cubs in 1983. He was also the winning pitcher.)

38) D – Colorado Rockies (The Mets had a 3-1 record against the Rockies, for a winning percentage of .750 for the season.)

39) B – 2 (In 1969 against the Baltimore Orioles and in 1986 against the Boston Red Sox)

40) A – Doc (Short for Dr. K, the K being the abbreviation for strikeouts by a pitcher)

41) C – Carlos Delgado (Carlos had nine RBIs in a seven-game series loss to the St. Louis Cardinals.)

42) B – 5 (1987 [823 runs], 1999 [853 runs], 2000 [807], 2006 [834 runs], and 2007 [804 runs])

43) A – Tom Seaver (Seaver pitched five complete one-hitters, one in 1969, 1970, 1971, 1972, and 1977.)

44) B – 4 (David Wright [3B], Carlos Beltran [CF], Francisco Rodriguez [P], and Johan Santana [P])

45) D – Carlos Beltran (Beltran hit three grand slams in July of 2006.)

46) B – 6 (The Mets had six selections in 2006: Carlos Beltran [CF], Paul Lo Duca [C], Tom Glavine [P], Pedro Martinez [P], Jose Reyes [SS], and David Wright [3B].)

47) A – 4 (Salty Parker [1967], Roy McMillan [1975], Frank Howard [1983], and Mike Cubbage [1991])

48) C – 37 (The pitching staff had 37 hits in 253 at-bats, for a .146 batting average.)

49) A – Buffalo Bisons (A member of the International League, they have been a Mets affiliate since 2009.)

50) B – 1967 (The New York Mets went 9-8 against the Atlanta Braves.)

Note: All answers valid as of the end of the 2009 season, unless otherwise indicated in the question itself.

1) What year did players names first appear on Mets team uniforms?

Answers begin on page 37

   A) 1964
   B) 1968
   C) 1979
   D) 1985

2) What jersey number did Mets great Keith Hernandez wear?

   A) #17
   B) #32
   C) #38
   D) #41

3) Not including 2010 inductees, how many players have been inducted into the National Baseball Hall of Fame with the Mets as their primary team?

   A) 1
   B) 3
   C) 5
   D) 7

4) Where did the Mets play their home games prior to Citi Field?

   A) Polo Grounds
   B) KeySpan Park
   C) The Meadowlands
   D) Shea Stadium

5) Did the Mets have a winning record on the road during the 2009 regular season?

    A) Yes
    B) No

6) How many times did New York sweep a series during the 2009 regular season?

    A) 2
    B) 4
    C) 6
    D) 7

7) When was the first time a Met hit 40 or more home runs in a single season?

    A) 1962
    B) 1976
    C) 1987
    D) 1996

8) Which of the following Mets players received the Cy Young Award three times?

    A) Dwight Gooden
    B) Al Leiter
    C) Tom Seaver
    D) David Cone

9) Since 1962, the Mets have had more winning seasons than losing seasons.

   A) True
   B) False

10) Which National League opponent have the Mets played the fewest times during the regular season?

   A) Milwaukee Brewers
   B) Colorado Rockies
   C) Arizona Diamondbacks
   D) Florida Marlins

11) What is the Mets' all-time winning percentage against the Phillies?

   A) .435
   B) .466
   C) .514
   D) .575

12) Since 1962, who is the only Met to lead the league in saves?

   A) Billy Wagner
   B) Armando Benitez
   C) John Franco
   D) Jesse Orosco

13) How many times have Mets pitchers been awarded the Cy Young Award?

    A) 2
    B) 4
    C) 6
    D) 8

14) When did the Mets first record a winning season in the National League?

    A) 1962
    B) 1964
    C) 1966
    D) 1969

15) What is the Mets' record for most hits as a team in a single season?

    A) 1,553
    B) 1,609
    C) 1,745
    D) 1,821

16) Has any Mets player ever hit greater than four grand slams in a single season?

    A) Yes
    B) No

17) What is the Mets' record for fewest errors as a team during the regular season?

    A) 68
    B) 73
    C) 78
    D) 81

18) Which Mets pitcher had the lowest ERA in 2009 (minimum 50 innings pitched)?

    A) John Maine
    B) Johan Santana
    C) Francisco Rodriguez
    D) Pedro Feliciano

19) Since 1962, how many Mets have been walked 125 or more times in a single season?

    A) 1
    B) 2
    C) 4
    D) 6

20) The Mets have won greater than 5,000 all-time regular-season games since joining the National League.

    A) True
    B) False

21) Which Mets player had the fewest number of at-bats per home run in his career?

A) Gary Carter
B) Darryl Strawberry
C) Mike Piazza
D) Dave Kingman

22) Which player holds the Mets career pinch-hit home run record?

A) Lee Mazzilli
B) Rusty Staub
C) Mark Carreon
D) Ed Kranepool

23) What was the salary paid by the Mets to Willie Mays in 1972?

A) $100,000
B) $175,000
C) $215,000
D) $250,000

24) What was the most recent year a Mets player received a Gold Glove Award?

A) 1999
B) 2006
C) 2008
D) 2009

25) Who was the Mets' manager in their first-ever winning season?

   A) Gil Hodges
   B) Yogi Berra
   C) Casey Stengel
   D) Wes Westrum

26) Who is the Mets' current pitching coach?

   A) Chip Hale
   B) Ray Ramirez
   C) Dan Warthen
   D) Howard Johnson

27) In the Mets-Yankees rivalry, the Mets have the most regular-season wins.

   A) True
   B) False

28) Who is the only Met to be named All-Star MVP?

   A) Jon Matlack
   B) Darryl Strawberry
   C) Ray Knight
   D) Edgardo Alfonzo

29) How many games did the Mets spend in first place during the 2009 season?

   A) 9
   B) 13
   C) 18
   D) 22

30) How many teams had a winning record against the Mets in the Mets' first-ever season?

   A) 4
   B) 6
   C) 8
   D) 9

31) Which award did Mets player Fernando Tatis receive in 2008?

   A) Roberto Clemente Award
   B) Branch Rickey Award
   C) Hank Aaron Award
   D) Comeback player of the Year Award

32) Against which National League team do the Mets have their highest all-time winning percentage (min. 500 games played)?

   A) Washington Nationals
   B) Chicago Cubs
   C) Philadelphia Phillies
   D) Cincinnati Reds

33) How many times have Mets pitchers recorded nineteen strikeouts in a single game?

    A) 1
    B) 2
    C) 3
    D) 5

34) Which year did the Mets first face the Dodgers in the postseason?

    A) 1969
    B) 1973
    C) 1988
    D) 2006

35) What is the Mets' record for most runs allowed in a single game?

    A) 21
    B) 26
    C) 28
    D) 29

36) Who was the only Mets player to wear jersey number 00?

    A) Tony Clark
    B) Turk Wendell
    C) Terry McDaniel
    D) Rey Ordonez

37) Who was New York's first-ever opponent in Citi Field?

    A) Milwaukee Brewers
    B) Washington Nationals
    C) San Diego Padres
    D) Cincinnati Reds

38) How many times has a Met hit for the cycle (single, double, triple, and home run in the same game)?

    A) 4
    B) 6
    C) 7
    D) 9

39) Which Mets pitcher holds the team record for lowest ERA in a season?

    A) Johan Santana
    B) Dwight Gooden
    C) Tom Seaver
    D) Bret Saberhagen

40) Has any Mets player had a batting average of .350 or higher for a single season?

    A) Yes
    B) No

41) Who holds the Mets' career record for stolen bases?

    A) Mookie Wilson
    B) Howard Johnson
    C) Lenny Dykstra
    D) Jose Reyes

42) How many Mets players have played over 1,500 career games?

    A) 1
    B) 2
    C) 3
    D) 5

43) What is the nickname of the AA team affiliated with the New York Mets?

    A) St. Lucie Mets
    B) Savannah Sand Gnats
    C) Binghamton Mets
    D) Brooklyn Cyclones

44) How many times have the Mets swept a postseason series?

    A) 1
    B) 2
    C) 3
    D) 4

45) Which Met had his jersey number retired, but is not a member of the National Baseball Hall of Fame?

    A)   Casey Stengel
    B)   Tom Seaver
    C)   Gary Carter
    D)   Gil Hodges

46) When did the Mets last host the All-Star Game?

    A)   1964
    B)   1972
    C)   1976
    D)   1996

47) Which Mets pitcher surrendered the most home runs in a single season?

    A)   Pete Harnisch
    B)   Roger Craig
    C)   Rick Reed
    D)   Pedro Astacio

48) How many times has a Mets manager won the National League Manager of the Year Award?

    A)   1
    B)   2
    C)   4
    D)   5

49) What decade did the Mets have the highest regular-season winning percentage?

    A) 1960s
    B) 1970s
    C) 1980s
    D) 2000s

50) What is the Mets' record for most hits by a pitcher in a season?

    A) 11
    B) 14
    C) 17
    D) 21

In the final game of the 1962 season, with the Mets losing 1-5 at Wrigley Field in Chicago, pinch-hitter Sammy Drake led off the top of the eighth with a single. Second baseman, and future Hall of Famer, Richie Ashburn followed with another single moving Drake to second. The result from the next at-bat symbolized the Mets' 120-loss season. Mets catcher Joe Pignatano hit a fly ball to the right side of the infield, where the Cubs second baseman made a running catch, flipped the ball to Ernie banks on first who then threw to Andre Rodgers covering second for an inning-ending triple play. Ironically, the three Mets players involved in the triple play never played another game with New York.

1) C – 1979 (The NL passed a rule in 1979 that required names on road uniforms. The Mets also placed names on their home jersey's at the same time.)

2) A – #17 (Keith played first base for the Mets from 1983-89. He had to change his number from 37, which he wore at St. Louis, because the Mets had retired it for former manager Casey Stengel.)

3) A – 1 (He was inducted into the Hall of Fame in 1992.)

4) D – Shea Stadium (The Mets played here from 1964-2008. The site now serves as a parking lot for Citi Field.)

5) B – No (The Mets went 29-52 on the road.)

6) C – 6 (The Mets had 2-0 regular-season series records against Atlanta and Philadelphia, and 3-0 records against Pittsburgh, San Francisco, Washington, and Houston.)

7) D – 1996 (Todd Hundley hit 41 home runs, which at that time was the most by a catcher in a single season. In 2006, Carlos Beltran also hit 41 home runs to tie Hundley for the most by a Met in a single season.)

8) C – Tom Seaver (Tom received these awards in 1969, 1973, and 1975.)

9) B – False (The Mets have only had 23 winning seasons in 48 years.)

10) A – Milwaukee Brewers (The Mets have played the Brewers a total of 82 times [52-30]. Milwaukee switched to the NL in 1998.)

11) B – .466 (NY is 380-435 all-time vs. the Phillies.)

12) C – John Franco (He led the league with 33 saves in 1990.)

13) B – 4 (Tom Seaver [1969, 1973, and 1975] and Dwight Gooden [1985] are the only Mets to be awarded a Cy Young Award.)

14) D – 1969 (The Mets had a record of 100-62 [.617] in their eighth season.)

15) A – 1,553 (This record was set in 1999 with 5,572 at-bats and a team batting average of .279.)

16) B – No (The record is 3 grand slams in a season and is held by John Milner [1976], Robin Ventura [1999], Mike Piazza [2000], and Carlos Beltran [2006].)

17) A – 68 (This record was set in 1999.)

18) D – Pedro Feliciano (Pedro had a 3.03 ERA in 59.1 innings.)

19) A – 1 (In 1999, John Olerud was walked 125 times.)

20) B – False (The Mets have an all-time record of 3,655-3,981, for a winning percentage of .479.)

21) D – Dave Kingman (Dave averaged 15.1 at-bats per home run from 1975-77 and 1981-83.)

22) C – Mark Carreon (Mark had eight pinch-hit home runs for the Mets from 1987-91.)

23) B – $175,000 (The Mets offered Willie $175,000 a year as a player and $50,000 a year as a coach after he retired.)

24) C – 2008 (David Wright was awarded his second and Carlos Beltran won his third Gold Glove Award.)

25) A – Gil Hodges (Gil managed the Mets to a 100-62 record and the World Series title in 1969.)
26) C – Dan Warthen (Dan was named the Mets pitching coach in June 2008.)
27) B – False (The Mets have a 30-42 record against the Yankees since interleague play started in 1997.)
28) A– Jon Matlack (Jon was co-MVP of the 1975 All-Star game along with Bill Madlock of the Chicago Cubs.)
29) B – 13 (The Mets spent a total of 13 games in first place in 2009. Their last day in first was May 29.)
30) C – 8 (Every team but the Chicago Cubs had a winning record against the Mets in 1962. The Mets had a 9-9 record against the Cubs.)
31) D – Comeback Player of the Year (Tatis averaged .297 in 92 games for the Mets in 2008 before separating his shoulder.)
32) A – Washington Nationals (The Mets are 351-331 all-time against the Nationals, for a .515 winning percentage. The Nationals were the Montreal Expos prior to moving to Washington after the 2004 season.)
33) B – 2 (David Cone recorded 19 strikeouts against the Phillies on Oct. 6, 1991, and Tom Seaver recorded 19 strikeouts against the Padres on April 22, 1970.)
34) C – 1988 (The Mets lost to the Dodgers [3-4] in the NL Championship Series despite winning their regular season match-up 10 games to one.)
35) B – 26 (NY lost 7-26 to the Phillies on June 11, 1985.)

36) A – Tony Clark (Tony wore #00 from April 5, 2003 to June 5, 2003. He switched to #52 after various kids asked him why he was wearing Mr. Met's number.)

37) C – San Diego Padres (The Mets lost 5-6 against the Padres on April 13, 2009. There were 41,944 fans in attendance for the first game in Citi Field, a single-game record for the season.)

38) D – 9 (Jim Hickman [1963], Tommie Agee [1970], Mike Phillips [1976], Keith Hernandez [1985 in 19 innings], Kevin McReynolds [1989], Alex Ochoa [1996], John Olerud [1997], Eric Valent [2004], and Jose Reyes [2006])

39) B – Dwight Gooden (Dwight set this record in 1985 with a 1.53 ERA.)

40) A – Yes (John Olerud had a batting average of .354 in 1998, recording 197 hits in 557 at-bats.)

41) D – Jose Reyes (He stole 301 bases with the Mets from 2003-09.)

42) A – 1 (Ed Kranepool played in 1,853 games for the Mets from 1962-79. "Steady Eddie" was 17 years old in 1962 and was the only Met to play in each of the franchise's first 18 seasons.)

43) C – Binghamton Mets (The Binghamton Mets have been affiliated with the New York Mets since 1991. They play in the Northern Division of the Eastern League and had a record of 54-86 in 2009.)

44) B – 2 (The Mets swept the Braves in the 1969 NL Championship Series and the Dodgers in the 2006 NL Divisional Series.)

45) D – Gil Hodges (Gil's #14 was retired on June 9, 1973. He played first base for the Mets in 1962-63 before managing the club from 1968-71. The #8, worn by Gary Carter, has not been retired nor issued to another player since Gary's retirement after the 1992 season.)

46) A – 1964 (The game was played at Shea Stadium with the NL winning 7-4. Second baseman Ron Hunt was the only Mets player on the roster.)

47) B – Roger Craig (He surrendered 35 home runs in 1962.)

48) A – 1 (Gil Hodges won the award in 1969.)

49) C – 1980s (The Mets finished the decade with an overall record of 816-743 [.523].)

50) D – 21 (He recorded 21 hits in the 1985 season.)

Note: All answers valid as of the end of the 2009 season, unless otherwise indicated in the question itself.

1) Who holds the Mets' record for most career grand slams?

Answers begin on page 56

    A)   Howard Johnson
    B)   Mike Piazza
    C)   Robin Ventura
    D)   Kevin McReynolds

2) While playing for which team did the Mets' Rusty Staub get his nickname "Le Grande Orange"?

    A)   Montreal Expos
    B)   Detroit Tigers
    C)   Texas Rangers
    D)   New York Yankees

3) When was the most recent season the Mets finished above .500?

    A)   2005
    B)   2006
    C)   2008
    D)   2009

4) Which Mets manager has the most career wins?

    A)   Willie Randolph
    B)   Davey Johnson
    C)   Gil Hodges
    D)   Bobby Valentine

5) Has any Mets pitcher ever thrown a no-hitter?

    A) Yes
    B) No

6) What are the most one-run games the Mets have won in a season?

    A) 23
    B) 36
    C) 41
    D) 52

7) What is the highest career winning percentage of a Mets pitcher with at least 100 career wins?

    A) .594
    B) .608
    C) .615
    D) .649

8) How many different pitchers did the Mets use during the 2009 regular season?

    A) 19
    B) 21
    C) 24
    D) 28

9) What is the Mets' all-time winning percentage against the Florida Marlins?

    A) .500
    B) .529
    C) .541
    D) .563

10) In 2009 Pedro Feliciano broke the Mets' record he set in 2008 for most games pitched in a season.

    A) True
    B) False

11) Which of the following Mets career records is not held by Darryl Strawberry?

    A) Home Runs
    B) RBIs
    C) Walks
    D) Total Bases

12) Which Mets manager has the highest career winning percentage in postseason play?

    A) Willie Randolph
    B) Gil Hodges
    C) Davey Johnson
    D) Bobby Valentine

13) What are the most errors the Mets have committed in a single season?

   A) 176
   B) 189
   C) 210
   D) 323

14) Which player never won a Gold Glove Award while playing for New York?

   A) Howard Johnson
   B) Doug Flynn
   C) Robin Ventura
   D) Bud Harrelson

15) Which Mets manager had the highest career winning percentage (minimum 3 seasons)?

   A) Bobby Valentine
   B) Davey Johnson
   C) Willie Randolph
   D) Gil Hodges

16) How many Mets players have recorded over 250 career stolen bases?

   A) 2
   B) 3
   C) 5
   D) 6

17) Who was the most recent Mets player to be named the National League Home Run Champion?

    A) Carlos Beltran
    B) Darryl Strawberry
    C) Dave Kingman
    D) Howard Johnson

18) Did any Mets pitcher hit a home run in 2009?

    A) Yes
    B) No

19) When was the most recent season the leading player for the Mets had fewer than 75 RBIs?

    A) 1994
    B) 2003
    C) 2006
    D) 2009

20) What is the current distance to the center field wall at Citi Field?

    A) 395'
    B) 401'
    C) 408'
    D) 413'

21) Who was the most recent Mets pitcher to lead the team in strikeouts, wins, innings pitched, and ERA in the same season?

    A) Johan Santana
    B) Tom Glavine
    C) Al Leiter
    D) Dwight Gooden

22) Who was the first-ever player named Mets team captain?

    A) John Franco
    B) Keith Hernandez
    C) Gary Carter
    D) Mookie Wilson

23) Willie Mays was the last player to wear #24 for the Mets.

    A) True
    B) False

24) When was the most recent season the Mets, as a team, had a batting average of .275 or higher?

    A) 1995
    B) 1999
    C) 2005
    D) 2007

25) Did Tom Seaver end his career with the Mets?

    A) Yes
    B) No

26) Who played in the most games for the Mets during the 2009 regular season?

    A) Luis Castillo
    B) Gary Sheffield
    C) Daniel Murphy
    D) David Wright

27) What are the most consecutive losses the Mets have ever had in one season?

    A) 12
    B) 13
    C) 15
    D) 17

28) Who did the Mets play on opening day in 2009?

    A) Cincinnati Reds
    B) Florida Marlins
    C) San Diego Padres
    D) Milwaukee Brewers

29) Has any Mets pitcher ever recorded 150 or more career saves?

    A) Yes
    B) No

30) What is the combined winning percentage of Mets mangers who lasted one season or less?

    A) .412
    B) .455
    C) .505
    D) .587

31) The Mets' Shea Stadium was the site of which major non-sporting event in 1965?

    A) Evil Knievel's Daredevil Show
    B) An appearance by Pope John Paul II
    C) A Beatles concert
    D) Summer Festival for Peace

32) Since 2000, who has hit the most home runs for the Mets?

    A) Carlos Delgado
    B) David Wright
    C) Carlos Beltran
    D) Mike Piazza

33) In 2007, against which team did the Mets' first two batters of the game hit home runs?

    A)   Atlanta Braves
    B)   Cincinnati Reds
    C)   St. Louis Cardinals
    D)   San Francisco Giants

34) What are the fewest losses by the Mets in one season?

    A)   43
    B)   48
    C)   54
    D)   62

35) Did any Met have greater than 250 assists in the 2009 regular season?

    A)   Yes
    B)   No

36) Which player holds the Mets' record for most at-bats in a single season?

    A)   Lance Johnson
    B)   Mookie Wilson
    C)   Tommie Agee
    D)   Jose Reyes

37) Who was New York's top draft pick in 2009?

    A)   Damien Magnifico
    B)   Steven Matz
    C)   Robert Shields
    D)   Darrell Ceciliani

38) Who holds the Mets' record for runs scored in a career?

    A)   Darryl Strawberry
    B)   Mookie Wilson
    C)   Howard Johnson
    D)   Edgardo Alfonzo

39) What are the most home runs hit by a Mets pitcher in a single season?

    A)   2
    B)   3
    C)   6
    D)   7

40) When was the most recent season the leading hitter for the Mets had a batting average below .300?

    A)   1995
    B)   2003
    C)   2004
    D)   2008

41) Who is the only Mets pitcher to win the National League Triple Crown?

    A)   Dwight Gooden
    B)   Tom Seaver
    C)   Jerry Koosman
    D)   Steve Trachsel

42) What is the Mets' record for most innings played in a single game?

    A)   18
    B)   20
    C)   23
    D)   25

43) Did a Mets pitcher ever win a Gold Glove Award?

    A)   Yes
    B)   No

44) Who was the most recent Met to hit an inside-the-park home run?

    A)   Damion Easley
    B)   Jose Reyes
    C)   Angel Pagan
    D)   Kazuo Matsui

45) How many Mets players have a career on-base percentage of .400 or higher?

    A) 1
    B) 3
    C) 4
    D) 6

46) What color are the seats at Citi Field?

    A) Red
    B) Dark Green
    C) Black
    D) Light Gray

47) In which inning did the Mets score the most runs throughout the 2009 regular season?

    A) 1st
    B) 2nd
    C) 4th
    D) 8th

48) How many Mets have won the Roberto Clemente Award?

    A) 1
    B) 3
    C) 4
    D) 6

49) The Mets had a better batting average against right-handed pitchers than left-handed pitchers in 2009.

    A) True
    B) False

50) Who hit the Mets' first home run in their first-ever game at Citi Field?

    A) David Wright
    B) Gary Sheffield
    C) Carlos Beltran
    D) Daniel Murphy

On the morning of the Mets' first game in franchise History in April of 1962, players and coaches were understandably excited to get to Busch Stadium to take on the St. Louis Cardinals. Unfortunately their season's misfortunes began before they ever left the hotel. They were at the Chase Hotel in downtown St. Louis when sixteen Mets piled into an elevator for the ride down to the lobby to catch the buses to the ballpark. The elevator suddenly stopped between floors, leaving them stuck in the elevator for two hours. This caused them to arrive late for their pre-game warm-ups. They went on to lose the game 4-11, and started their inaugural season 0-9.

1) B – Mike Piazza (He hit 6 grand slams as a Met [1998-2005].)

2) A – Montreal Expos (Rusty spent three seasons in Montreal, before joining the Mets in 1972. He was given the nickname because of his red hair.)

3) C – 2008 (The Mets finished the season 89-73, for a .549 winning percentage.)

4) B – Davey Johnson (He led the Mets to 595 wins from 1984-90.)

5) B – No (There have been 32 one-hitters in Mets history, but not a single no-hitter.)

6) C – 41 (In 1969, the Mets were 41-23 in one-run games.)

7) D – .649 (Dwight Gooden had a career record of 157-85.)

8) C – 24 (Only 13 of them pitched 50 innings or more.)

9) B – .529 (The Mets are 137-122 all-time against the Marlins.)

10) A – True (Pedro appeared in 88 games for the Mets in 2009, which was two more than his record in 2008.)

11) D – Total Bases (This career record is held by Ed Kranepool [2,047]. Darryl holds career records for home runs [252], RBIs [733], and walks [580].)

12) B – Gil Hodges (He had a career postseason record of 7-1 [.875].)

13) C – 210 (This record was set and tied in the Mets' first two seasons [1962 and 1963].)

14) A – Howard Johnson (Six Mets infielders have won Gold Gloves: Bud Harrelson [1971], Doug Flynn [1980], Keith Hernandez [1983, 1984, 1985, 1986, 1987, and 1988], Rey Ordonez [1997, 1998, and 1999], Robin Ventura [1999], and David Wright [2007 and 2008].)

15) B – Davey Johnson (Johnson coached the Mets from 1984-90. He had a winning percentage of .588 in his seven years with the Mets.)

16) A – 2 (Jose Reyes [301] and Mookie Wilson [281])

17) D – Howard Johnson (He hit 38 home runs in 1991.)

18) B – No (Mets pitchers had 37 hits in 2009, including four doubles and one triple, but no home runs.)

19) D – 2009 (David Wright led the team with 72 RBIs.)

20) C – 408' (Direct center field was 410' at Shea Stadium.)

21) A – Johan Santana (In 2008, Santana led the team in strikeouts [206], wins [16], innings pitched [234.1], and ERA [2.53].)

22) B – Keith Hernandez (All-time the Mets have had only three team captains: Keith Hernandez [1987-89], Gary Carter [1988-89], and John Franco [2001-04].)

23) B – False (#24 has only been issued to two players since Willie Mays retired, Kelvin Torve in 1990, by mistake, and Rickey Henderson as a player from 1999-2000 and as a coach in 2007.)

24) D – 2007 (The Mets had a team batting average of .275.)

25) B – No (Tom finished his career with the Boston Red Sox in 1986.)

26) C – Daniel Murphy (Daniel played in 155 games.)

27) D – 17 (The Mets lost every game from May 21, 1962 through June 6, 1962.)

28) A – Cincinnati Reds (With the Mets leading, Francisco Rodriguez got Ramon Hernandez to strike out swinging to seal a Mets win [2-1].)

29) A – Yes (John Franco recorded 276 saves from 1990-2004 and Armando Benitez recorded 160 saves from 1999-2003.)

30) B – .455 (Mets managers who lasted one season or less had a combined record of 85-102.)

31) C – A Beatles concert (The Beatles opened their 1965 North American tour to a record crowd of 55,600.)

32) D – Mike Piazza (Mike hit 157 of his 220 home runs with the Mets from 2000-2005.)

33) B – Cincinnati Reds (On July 12, 2007, Jose Reyes and Ruben Gotay had back-to-back home runs in the first two at-bats for the Mets. The Mets went on to win 3-2.)

34) C – 54 (The Mets had 54 losses in 1986, for a winning percentage of .667.)

35) A – Yes (Luis Castillo led the team with 344 assists.)

36) D – Jose Reyes (He had 696 at-bats in 2005.)

37) B – Steven Matz (Steven is a left-handed pitcher from Ward Melville high school in East Setauket, N.Y. The Mets selected him in the second round, the 72nd overall pick. The Mets lost their first-round pick of 2009 as compensation to the Angeles for signing free agent Francisco Rodriguez.)

38) A – Darryl Strawberry (He scored a career 662 runs with the Mets from 1983-90.)

39) B – 3 (Tom Seaver [1972] and Walt Terrell [1983] both hit three home runs in a single season.)

40) C – 2004 (Kazuo Matsui led the team with a .272 batting average.)

41) A – Dwight Gooden (In 1985 Dwight led the league in wins [24], ERA [1.53], and strikeouts [268].)

42) D – 25 (The Mets lost 3-4 to the Cardinals on Sept. 11, 1974, in a game that took 7 hours and 4 minutes to complete.)

43) A – Yes (Ron Darling [1989] is the only Mets pitcher to receive a Gold Glove.)

44) C – Angel Pagan (Pagan recorded the first inside-the park home run at Citi Field against the Phillies on Aug. 23, 2009.)

45) A – 1 (John Olerud had a .425 on-base percentage from 1997-99.)

46) B – Dark Green (The color is a tribute to the New York Metropolitans' first home, the Polo Grounds.)

47) C – 4th (The Mets scored 90 total runs in the 4th inning. The next highest was 87 total runs in the first.)

48) B – 3 (Gary Carter [1989], Al Leiter [2000], and Carlos Delgado [2006] all received the award. It is given annually to MLB players who exemplify sportsmanship and make positive contributions to their community.)

49) B – False (The Mets batted .269 against right-handed pitchers and .273 against left-handed pitchers.)

50) A – David Wright (In the bottom of the fifth with two runners on and two outs, David hit a 3-2 pitch to deep left field for a three-run home run.)

Note: All answers valid as of the end of the 2009 season, unless otherwise indicated in the question itself.

1) Which team did Jerry Manuel manage before joining the Mets organization?

Answers begin on page 75

    A) Oakland Athletics
    B) Chicago White Sox
    C) Detroit Tigers
    D) California Angels

2) In which country did the Mets and Expos play a four-game series in 2003?

    A) England
    B) Mexico
    C) Puerto Rico
    D) Dominican Republic

3) Which pitcher has the most career wins against the Mets?

    A) Greg Maddux
    B) Bob Gibson
    C) Steve Carlton
    D) Phil Niekro

4) Where is the Mets' Latin Baseball camp located?

    A) Mexico
    B) Puerto Rico
    C) Venezuela
    D) Dominican Republic

5) In 2004, Mets shortstop Kazuo Matsui hit a home run on the first pitch of his first major league at-bat.

    A) True
    B) False

6) How many Mets have hit 30 home runs and stole 30 bases in the same season?

    A) 1
    B) 2
    C) 3
    D) 5

7) What is the Mets' record for most consecutive winning seasons?

    A) 5
    B) 7
    C) 9
    D) 11

8) Which team have the Mets played the greatest number of times?

    A) Pittsburgh Pirates
    B) St. Louis Cardinals
    C) Chicago Cubs
    D) Philadelphia Phillies

9) What year did Ralph Kiner start his Mets broadcasting career?

    A) 1962
    B) 1965
    C) 1971
    D) 1980

10) Which Mets outfielder won the most Gold Glove Awards?

    A) Tommie Agee
    B) Cleon Jones
    C) Carlos Beltran
    D) Darryl Strawberry

11) What team did Joe Torre manage after the Mets?

    A) Atlanta Braves
    B) Los Angeles Dodgers
    C) New York Yankees
    D) St. Louis Cardinals

12) Has any Mets player led the league in runs scored in a single season?

    A) Yes
    B) No

13) Which Mets player was nicknamed "The Kid"?

   A) David Cone
   B) Tug McGraw
   C) Gary Carter
   D) Willie Mays

14) Which item belonging to Met Julio Franco is now an artifact in the National Baseball Hall of Fame?

   A) Glove
   B) Bat
   C) Jersey
   D) Spikes

15) What is the name of the series between the Mets and the Yankees?

   A) Trolley Series
   B) Freeway Series
   C) Crosstown Classic
   D) Subway Series

16) Which Met had the first-ever hit at Citi Field?

   A) Carlos Delgado
   B) Jose Reyes
   C) David Wright
   D) Ryan Church

17) How many Mets batters won the National League Triple Crown?

   A) 0
   B) 1
   C) 2
   D) 3

18) When was the most recent season the Mets failed to hit 100 or more team home runs?

   A) 1992
   B) 1998
   C) 2003
   D) 2009

19) Where do the Mets hold spring training?

   A) Glendale, Ariz.
   B) Port St. Lucie, Fla.
   C) Sarasota, Fla.
   D) Clearwater, Fla.

20) Who is the only Mets pitcher to lead the team in strikeouts for ten consecutive years?

   A) Al Leiter
   B) Dwight Gooden
   C) Tom Seaver
   D) John Franco

21) All-time, how many managers have the Mets had?

    A) 15
    B) 19
    C) 24
    D) 27

22) Who threw out the ceremonial first pitch for the first-ever game at Citi Field?

    A) Mike Bloomberg
    B) Fred Wilpon
    C) President George H. W. Bush
    D) Tom Seaver

23) Which Mets manager had the second highest winning percentage (minimum three seasons)?

    A) Gil Hodges
    B) Willie Randolph
    C) Bobby Valentine
    D) Yogi Berra

24) Did the Mets win every game in 2009 when hitting three or more home runs?

    A) Yes
    B) No

25) What is the Mets' record for the most times a single
player has been hit by pitch in a season?

    A) 9
    B) 11
    C) 13
    D) 19

26) Who was the Mets' lead-off batter for the first 33 games
of 2009?

    A) Jose Reyes
    B) Angel Pagan
    C) Carlos Beltran
    D) Luis Castillo

27) What year was the Mets' first-ever home night game in
Shea Stadium?

    A) 1963
    B) 1964
    C) 1966
    D) 1968

28) Which of the following players won the Baseball America
Minor League Player of the Year Award twice?

    A) Jose Reyes
    B) Dwight Gooden
    C) Darryl Strawberry
    D) Gregg Jefferies

29) What decade did the Mets have the lowest winning percentage?

    A) 1960s
    B) 1970s
    C) 1990s
    D) 2000s

30) When was the most recent season the Mets total home attendance was less than three million?

    A) 1997
    B) 2000
    C) 2003
    D) 2005

31) How many times have the Mets finished in first place and failed to win the World Series?

    A) 1
    B) 3
    C) 4
    D) 6

32) What is the lowest team batting average the Mets ever had in a single season?

    A) .219
    B) .225
    C) .235
    D) .240

33) Which Mets pitcher recorded the second most career strikeouts?

    A)   Dave Cone
    B)   Jerry Koosman
    C)   Dwight Gooden
    D)   Ron Darling

34) How many Mets pitchers have won the National League Relief Man of the Year Award?

    A)   1
    B)   2
    C)   3
    D)   5

35) How many Mets have won National League Rookie of the Year?

    A)   2
    B)   3
    C)   4
    D)   6

36) How many times has New York won the first game in a postseason series?

    A)   3
    B)   6
    C)   7
    D)   9

Metsology Trivia Challenge

37) What is the Mets' record for most runs scored in the first inning of a game?

    A) 5
    B) 6
    C) 7
    D) 9

38) What was the lowest regular-season winning percentage of a Mets World Series Championship team?

    A) .568
    B) .617
    C) .625
    D) .667

39) What is the Mets' record for most pitchers used in a single nine-inning game?

    A) 6
    B) 7
    C) 8
    D) 10

40) Have the Mets ever had two brothers start in the same game?

    A) Yes
    B) No

41) What is the nickname of the Mets' single A affiliate located in Brooklyn, N.Y.?

    A) Cyclones
    B) Sand Gnats
    C) Coneys
    D) Brooklynites

42) Who was the most recent Mets player to lead the National League in hits in a season?

    A) David Wright
    B) Lance Johnson
    C) Jose Reyes
    D) Ty Wigginton

43) What term did Mets radio play-by-play announcer Bob Murphy use to begin his game recap following a win?

    A) Good Mets' Report
    B) Happy Recap
    C) Now for the good news
    D) Amazin' Mets Report

44) What was the highest winning percentage of a Mets manager who lasted one season or less?

    A) .431
    B) .448
    C) .491
    D) .534

45) When was the most recent season the Mets failed to score 500 runs?

    A)   1981
    B)   1983
    C)   1994
    D)   2003

46) Who was the most recent Met to lead the National League in RBIs?

    A)   Mike Cameron
    B)   David Wright
    C)   Mike Piazza
    D)   Lance Johnson

47) All-time, how many no-hitters have been thrown against the Mets (includes perfect games)?

    A)   3
    B)   4
    C)   7
    D)   9

48) How many times have the Mets won 100 or more games in a season without winning the World Series?

    A)   1
    B)   2
    C)   3
    D)   5

49) Of the ten teenagers who played for the Mets, who was the youngest?

    A)   Jose Reyes
    B)   Ed Kranepool
    C)   Tim Foli
    D)   Nolan Ryan

50) Has a Mets player ever won the Home Run Derby at the MLB All-Star Game?

    A)   Yes
    B)   No

On Sept. 9, 1969, the Mets and Cubs faced off at Shea Stadium in what has become known as the "Black Cat" game. The Mets were trailing the division-leading Cubs by 1.5 games with only 24 games left to play in the season. While Cub's third baseman Ron Santo warmed up in the on-deck circle, a black cat came out from under the stands near the Cubs' dugout. It circled Santo and walked in front of the Cubs' dugout, staring at all the players before disappearing back under the stands. The Mets defeated the Cubs 7-1 that day, and would go on to win the division eight games ahead of the cursed Cubbies.

1) B – Chicago White Sox (Jerry managed the White Sox to a 500-471 record from 1998-2003.)

2) C – Puerto Rico (This marked the first time that New York played in Puerto Rico. The Mets were swept by the Expos in the series.)

3) A – Greg Maddux (He has a 35-19 record vs. the Mets.)

4) D – Dominican Republic (The Mets opened the "New York Mets Dominican Baseball Academy" in the summer of 2008. The field is a replica of the Mets' Citi Field.)

5) A – True (Matsui hit the first pitch of the game on April 6, 2004, off of Russ Ortiz.)

6) C – 3 (Howard Johnson accomplished this 3 times: 1987 [36 HR and 32 SB], 1989 [36 HR and 41 SB], and 1991 [38 HR and 30 SB]. The other two players are Darryl Strawberry in 1987 [39 HR and 36 SB] and David Wright in 2007 [30 HR and 34 SB].)

7) B – 7 (The Mets had winning seasons from 1984-90 compiling a record of 666-466 [.588].)

8) D – Philadelphia Phillies (The Mets have played the Phillies 816 times and have a record of 380-435-1, for a .466 winning percentage.)

9) A – 1962 (Ralph joined the Mets broadcast team after a 10-year playing career that earned him election into the Hall of Fame in 1975. Ralph's home run calls, "It is gone, goodbye." or "That ball is gone, goodbye." have become signature phrases in baseball.)

10) C – Carlos Beltran (Carlos won Gold Glove Awards three times as an outfielder [2006-08].)

11) A – Atlanta Braves (Joe managed the Mets from 1977-81, all losing seasons. He then went to the Braves where they won their first 13 games of the 1982 season.)

12) B – No (Carlos Beltran finished second in runs scored in 2008 with 116, just one ahead of David Wrights' 115. They both finished behind Hanley Ramirez of Florida who had 125.)

13) C – Gary Carter (Mets catcher from 1985-89, Gary received "The Kid" nickname from teammates while playing for the Expos from 1974-84 and 1992.)

14) B – Bat (Julio hit a home run against San Diego on April 20, 2006, to become the oldest major leaguer to hit a home run. He was 47 years and 240 days old at the time.)

15) D – Subway Series (The interleague series between the Mets and the Yankees is referred to as the Subway Series. The stadiums of both teams are directly accessible by subway.)

16) C – David Wright (David hit a 0-1 pitch from San Diego's Walter Silva down the RF line for a double.)

17) A – 0 (No Mets batter has won the NL Triple Crown.)

18) D – 2009 (The Mets hit 95 HRs as a team in 2009.)

19) B – Port St. Lucie (The Mets play in the Grapefruit League [along with 15 other MLB teams] at Tradition Field.)

20) C – Tom Seaver (Seaver led the Mets in strikeouts 11 seasons [1967-76 and 1983].)

21) B – 19 (From Casey Stengel [1962-65] to Jerry Manuel [2008-present])

22) D – Tom Seaver (Tom threw the ceremonial first pitch and Mike Piazza caught it, just like the last pitch at Shea Stadium.)

23) B – Willie Randolph (Randolph managed the Mets from 2005-08 and led the team to a record of 302-253, for a .544 winning percentage.)

24) A – Yes (The Mets hit three home runs in a game three times in 2009. They won all of those games.)

25) C – 13 (Both Ron Hunt [1963] and John Olerud [1997] were hit by pitch 13 times in a single season.)

26) A – Jose Reyes (Reyes only played in 36 games before getting injured.)

27) B – 1964 (The first night game at Shea Stadium was played against Cincinnati on May 6, 1964. The Mets lost 4-12 to the Reds.)

28) D – Gregg Jefferies (Gregg won the Baseball America Minor League Player of the Year Award in 1986 and 1987 when he averaged .353 and .367 respectively in the Mets' minor league organization.)

29) A – 1960s (The Mets finished the decade with a record of 494-799, for a .382 winning percentage.)

30) D – 2005 (Total home attendance was 2,829,931 in 81 games for an average of 34,937 per game.)

31) B – 3 (1973, 1988, and 2006)

32) A – .219 (1,168 hits in 5,336 at-bats in 1962)

33) C – Dwight Gooden (He recorded 1,875 career strikeouts with the Mets [1984-94]. The leader in career strikeouts is Tom Seaver [1967-77 and 1983] with 2,541.)

34) B – 2 (John Franco [1990] & Armando Benitez [2001])

35) C – 4 (Tom Seaver [1967], Jon Matlack [1972], Darryl Strawberry [1983], and Dwight Gooden [1984])

36) B – 6 (The Mets won six out of 14 postseason series opening games.)

37) D – 9 (The Mets set this record against the Giants on Aug. 16, 1988, at Candlestick Park.)

38) B – .617 (NY finished with a 100-62 record in 1969.)

39) C – 8 (The Mets used eight pitchers in a nine-inning game six times. The most recent was against the Florida Marlins on Sept. 26, 2008.)

40) A – Yes (On Sept. 25, 2003, Mets pitcher Tom Glavine made his final start of the year, while his younger brother Mike made his first and only major league start of his career at first base.)

41) A – Cyclones (The Brooklyn Cyclones have been affiliated with the Mets since 2001.)

42) C – Jose Reyes (He led the National League in 2008 with 204 hits.)

43) B – Happy Recap (Renowned Mets broadcaster Bob Murphy [with the Mets from 1962-2003] would mention a Happy Recap after a Mets win and just a Recap after a Mets loss.)

44) C – .491 (Roy McMillan had this winning percentage after a 26-27 record in 1975.)

45) A – 1981 (The Mets scored 348 runs in the strike-shortened season.)

46) D – Lance Johnson (He led the National League with 117 RBIs in 1991.)

47) C – 7 (There have been 6 no-hitters and 1 perfect game thrown against the Mets, the most recent was a no-hitter by Houston's Darryl Kile in 1993.)

48) A – 1 (1988 [100-60])

49) B – Ed Kranepool (He was 17 years, 10 months, and 14 days at the time of his first game with the Mets [Sept. 22, 1962].)

50) A – Yes (Darryl Strawberry tied Wally Joyner of the California Angels for the top spot in the All-Star game held at the Astrodome in 1986.)

Note: All answers valid as of the end of the 2009 season, unless otherwise indicated in the question itself.

1) Which Met hit the longest home run in Shea Stadium history?

Answers begin on page 83

  A) Dave Kingman
  B) Darryl Strawberry
  C) Tommie Agee
  D) Mo Vaughn

2) All-time, how many World Series games have the Mets lost by a single run?

  A) 4
  B) 6
  C) 7
  D) 8

3) How many overall no. 1 draft picks have the Mets had?

  A) 5
  B) 8
  C) 9
  D) 11

4) Did Casey Stengel win his last-ever game as a Mets manager?

  A) Yes
  B) No

5) What are the most wins by a Mets pitcher in a single season?

    A) 22
    B) 23
    C) 25
    D) 26

6) Who holds the Mets' record for most doubles in a season?

    A) David Wright
    B) Bernard Gilkey
    C) Howard Johnson
    D) Edgardo Alfonzo

7) How many times has New York finished the regular season in first place?

    A) 5
    B) 6
    C) 8
    D) 9

8) The Mets have hit greater than 5,000 home runs in their history.

    A) True
    B) False

9) Off of which pitcher did Mookie Wilson hit a ground ball that went though first baseman Bill Buckner's legs in Game 6 of the 1986 World Series?

    A) Paxton Crawford
    B) Calvin Schiraldi
    C) Bob Stanley
    D) Al Nipper

10) What is the Mets' record for most runs scored in a nine-inning game?

    A) 17
    B) 19
    C) 21
    D) 23

1) C – Tommie Agee (He hit the only fair ball to reach the third deck in Shea Stadium history in 1969.)

2) B – 6 (The Mets lost a total of 12 World Series games, six of them by a single run.)

3) A – 5 (The last overall no. 1 pick the Mets had was RHP Paul Wilson in 1994.)

4) B – No (The Mets lost to the Phillies [5-1] on July 24, 1965. Casey broke his hip from a fall later that night, leading to his retirement from baseball.)

5) C – 25 (Tom Seaver recorded 25 wins in 1969.)

6) B – Bernard Gilkey (He hit 44 doubles in 1996.)

7) A – 5 (1969, 1973, 1986, 1988, and 2006)

8) A – True (The 5,000th Met home run came off the bat of Jason Phillips on Aug. 30, 2003. To date the Mets have 6,010 all-time home runs.)

9) C – Bob Stanley (Ray Knight scored from third for the winning run in the bottom of the 10th.)

10) D – 23 (The Mets beat the Cubs 23-10 on Aug. 16, 1987.)

Note: All answers valid as of the end of the 2009 season, unless otherwise indicated in the question itself.

Player / Team Score Sheet

Name:_____

Spring Training			Regular Season			Postseason			Championship Series			Extra Innings Bonus	
1	26		1	26		1	26		1	26		1	
2	27		2	27		2	27		2	27		2	
3	28		3	28		3	28		3	28		3	
4	29		4	29		4	29		4	29		4	
5	30		5	30		5	30		5	30		5	
6	31		6	31		6	31		6	31		6	
7	32		7	32		7	32		7	32		7	
8	33		8	33		8	33		8	33		8	
9	34		9	34		9	34		9	34		9	
10	35		10	35		10	35		10	35		10	
11	36		11	36		11	36		11	36			
12	37		12	37		12	37		12	37			
13	38		13	38		13	38		13	38			
14	39		14	39		14	39		14	39			
15	40		15	40		15	40		15	40			
16	41		16	41		16	41		16	41			
17	42		17	42		17	42		17	42			
18	43		18	43		18	43		18	43			
19	44		19	44		19	44		19	44			
20	45		20	45		20	45		20	45			
21	46		21	46		21	46		21	46			
22	47		22	47		22	47		22	47			
23	48		23	48		23	48		23	48			
24	49		24	49		24	49		24	49			
25	50		25	50		25	50		25	50			

___x 1 =____   ___x 2 =____   ___x 3 =____   ___x 4 =____   ___x 4 =____

Multiply total number correct by point value/quarter to calculate totals for each quarter.

Add total of all quarters below.

Total Points:_____

Thank you for playing *Metsology Trivia Challenge*.

Additional score sheets are available at:
www.TriviaGameBooks.com

Player / Team Score Sheet

Name:_____

Spring Training			Regular Season			Postseason			Championship Series			Extra Innings Bonus	
1	26		1	26		1	26		1	26		1	
2	27		2	27		2	27		2	27		2	
3	28		3	28		3	28		3	28		3	
4	29		4	29		4	29		4	29		4	
5	30		5	30		5	30		5	30		5	
6	31		6	31		6	31		6	31		6	
7	32		7	32		7	32		7	32		7	
8	33		8	33		8	33		8	33		8	
9	34		9	34		9	34		9	34		9	
10	35		10	35		10	35		10	35		10	
11	36		11	36		11	36		11	36			
12	37		12	37		12	37		12	37			
13	38		13	38		13	38		13	38			
14	39		14	39		14	39		14	39			
15	40		15	40		15	40		15	40			
16	41		16	41		16	41		16	41			
17	42		17	42		17	42		17	42			
18	43		18	43		18	43		18	43			
19	44		19	44		19	44		19	44			
20	45		20	45		20	45		20	45			
21	46		21	46		21	46		21	46			
22	47		22	47		22	47		22	47			
23	48		23	48		23	48		23	48			
24	49		24	49		24	49		24	49			
25	50		25	50		25	50		25	50			
___ x 1 = ___			___ x 2 = ___			___ x 3 = ___			___ x 4 = ___			___ x 4 = ___	

Multiply total number correct by point value/quarter to calculate totals for each quarter.

Add total of all quarters below.

Total Points:_____

Thank you for playing *Metsology Trivia Challenge*.

Additional score sheets are available at:
www.TriviaGameBooks.com